HEROES AND WARRIORS

MACBETH

SCOTLAND'S WARRIOR KING

BOB STEWART

Plates by JAMES FIELD

Firebird Books

28,658

First published in the UK 1988 by Firebird Books

Copyright © 1988 Firebird Books Ltd, P.O. Box 327, Poole, Dorset BH15 2RG
Text copyright © 1988 R. J. Stewart

Distributed in the United States by
Sterling Publishing Co, Inc,
2 Park Avenue, New York, NY 10016

Distributed in Australia by
Capricorn Link (Australia) Pty Ltd
P.O. Box 665, Lane Cove, NSW 2066

British Library Cataloguing in Publication Data

Stewart, Bob
   Macbeth : Scotland's warrior king.——(Heroes and warriors series).
   1. Macbeth, *King of Scotland* 2. Scotland——Kings and rulers——Biography
   I. Title II. Series
   941.101'0924   DA778.8

ISBN 1 85314 000 7

Series editor Stuart Booth
Designed by Kathryn S.A. Booth
Typeset by Colset Private Limited, Singapore
Colour separation by Kingfisher Facsimile
Colour printed by Butler and Tanner, Frome and London
Printed in Great Britain by Richard Clay Ltd, Chichester, Sussex

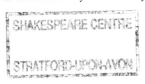

MACBETH

SCOTLAND'S WARRIOR KING

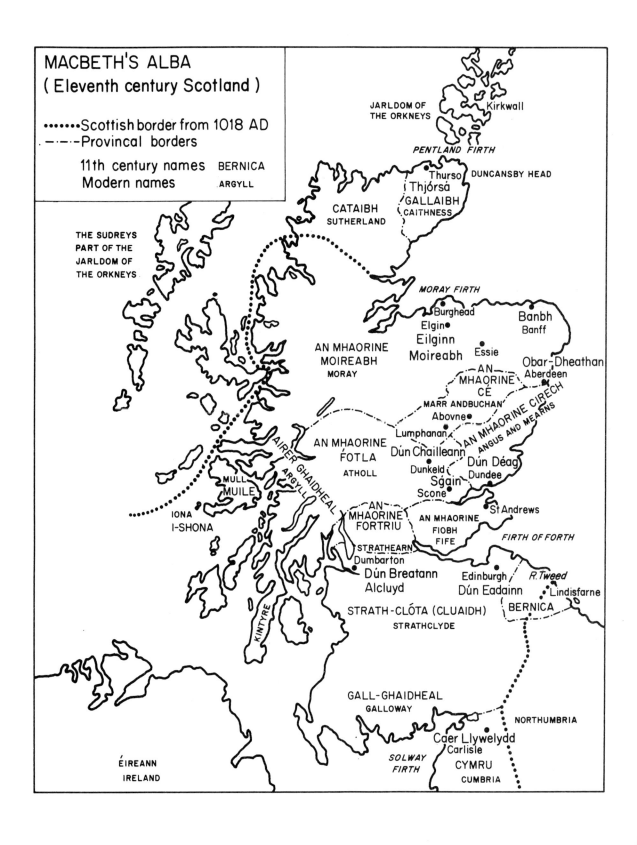

The Real Macbeth

Macbeth was High King of Scotland from 1040–1057. His life, as misrepresented by chronicles written as much as three centuries after his death, was the foundation for a major character in a Shakespeare play which in turn generated many other works of creative fiction. There is a version by Guiseppe Verdi as a full opera composed in 1847. A further musical work was composed by Richard Strauss in 1887 and of course many film and stage variants now exist on the basic theme as created by Shakespeare. The most recent and perhaps the best film version to date is that directed by Roman Polanski, though it must be said that no film has yet been made telling the historical and true story of Macbeth. A number of books, mainly fiction, have been inspired by the tale of Macbeth. Perhaps the most comprehensive and historical of these is Dorothy Dunnet's epic novel *King Hereafter*.

The period in which Macbeth rose to power, the eleventh century, was extremely complex. Kings rose and fell across Europe, often with very short disputed reigns; popes and archbishops were made and unmade; savage Norse raiders carved out territories for themselves by the sword, while in the south their distant cousins the Normans were gradually becoming the great new military power of the century.

An enormous book would be needed to cover fully such a vast tapestry of politics, social change and religion, all woven inextricably together. Indeed, many detailed and lengthy historical sources and reference works are necessary to even begin to approach the true Macbeth. And it may well come as a surprise to the modern reader to discover that this man was almost the exact opposite of the character so powerfully drawn by William Shakespeare.

Much of the history of Macbeth can only be understood in the broad complex context of English and European history, as this context had profound effects upon Alba (Scotland). So, in concentrating upon the central hero, his culture, his battles – and his final end – a great mass of European history is inevitably omitted. But wherever immediate politics or cultural background help us to understand Macbeth, these are included.

It is not possible to write about Macbeth without considering, at least by comparison, the remarkable work of literature created by William

Shakespeare six centuries after the true historical period. Some of the major comparisons, such as the characters of Duncan and Macbeth, are included when the kingship and the succession by election are discussed. The simple fact that Scottish High Kings were elected is central to a proper understanding of the period; this concept was quite alien to later writers, and probably incomprehensible to Shakespeare. The world famous play is a study of evil and corruption: the fact that it revolves around an entirely fabricated and non-historical Macbeth is almost irrelevent – until we decide to examine the true Macbeth.

There is no intention here of debunking or discrediting Shakespeare; any such attempt would be absurd and unsuccessful. Yet the play *Macbeth* has so strongly, coloured our general image of that Scottish king, the first to try and unify Scotland, that we must regard the historical Macbeth as a quite different from the fictional one. The two are only superficially related; one is a character profoundly drawn in one of the greatest dramas ever written; the other is a Scottish king whose reign marked a turning point in history. They share a name and some general background, but otherwise there is little in common between them.

Although the actual facts of Macbeth's reign agree in some respects with those dramatised by Shakespeare, history offers us a very different picture of the true Macbeth. He is normally regarded as a usurper, a tyrant, and an intolerable oppressor of his subjects. In reality, whilst he was indeed the murderer of his predecessor, this was in circumstances which made the crime nothing unusual for the historical period.

On seizing the throne, Macbeth used his power well, and was an effective and competent king; certainly not the crazed tyrant suggested in the world famous play. The difference between the true Macbeth and the fictitious figure of drama can be understood by looking further at his background. Also we have to delve into the changes of attitude and the political influence which eventually generated the Shakespearean picture.

During the reign of his predecessor Duncan, Macbeth was the Mormaer of Ross and Moray; he ruled over a large area of Scotland, consisting of all the land to the north of the Moray Firth and Loch Ness, in addition to territories in the Orkneys.

Duncan set out to subdue the independent chiefs of the north, and while engaged in this campaign was killed, either by Macbeth or on his orders. His death occurred in a place known as Bothgowan, which has been interpreted as meaning 'in a smith's hut'. This killing, eventually to be immortalised by Shakespeare in his retelling of historical chronicles, is likely to have taken place near Elgin, in the year 1039.

But the detailed history of this murder is more complex. Macbeth is said to have been encouraged by his wife Gruach (pronounced 'Gro-ah'), who was a granddaughter of the earlier King Kenneth III. Kenneth had been murdered and succeeded by Duncan's grandfather, Malcom II. The pattern of death and succession was not merely limited to Macbeth and Duncan; it had an immedi-

6

A nineteenth century production of Macbeth.

ate family background of revenge and politics. Furthermore, it echoed the ancient Celtic custom by which kingship was not hereditary, but elective. In very primal Celtic cultures, kings were established through magical or pagan religious processes; one of these was through combat between chosen individuals. Such combats had been transformed into political warfare by the time of Macbeth in the eleventh century, but originated in a purely magical tradition, within which the people would follow the elected or chosen king regardless. In fact, it was this misunderstanding of the ancient system of kingship that led later English chroniclers to treat Macbeth as a usurping tyrant, a theme to be taken up centuries later by Shakespeare. England had already moved towards a hereditary monarchy by the eleventh century, relying on political patterns rather different from those still prevailing in Scotland.

Macbeth reigned for seventeen years after the death of Duncan, and as has been said, ruled well. He is the first king of Scotland who is mentioned as benefactor of the church (as religion had been decentralised previously under the non-political Celtic church). Macbeth, however, favoured the growing Roman Church and for obvious political reasons offered his services to the Pope, being the first Scottish king to do so.

Macbeth's dominions were more extensive than those of any previous Scottish king, embracing the whole of what is now called Scotland, other than Orkney, Caithness and Sutherland, and parts of the Hebrides. These regions were ruled by Earl Thorfinn, a Norse jarl, who we shall return to repeatedly in our examination of the life of Macbeth. Scotland extended further south during Macbeth's reign than it does today, though this extension was to be lost by Malcolm III, who took the throne by force from Macbeth and his stepson Lulach.

Horse gear from Viking boat burial at Balladoole in the Isle of Man. Viking culture was absorbed into the existing Celtic backgrounds of Orkney, the Isle of Man and parts of Ireland, including Dublin.

Shakespeare took his version of the history from the Chronicles of Holinshed, or perhaps from those of Hector Boece. These sources were familiar only with the concept of hereditary monarchy; if we trace the lineage of the kings of Scotland *backwards* Macbeth might be termed a 'usurper' for after him the throne definitely became a hereditary property. It is this significant role as a figure at the crossroads of Scottish history that should be rightly accorded to the historical Macbeth.

Macbeth the Man

Macbeth is described by chroniclers in complimentary terms, very different from the literary image of a mad, despotic murderer. Contemporary writers such as Marianus Scotus, Tighernach, and Duan Albanach variously call Macbeth 'ruddy of countenance, tall with yellow hair'; 'a liberal king . . . fair and tall'; 'the red king . . .'. St Berchan called him a handsome youth, so there can be little doubt that his appearance was comely.

Doada, Macbeth's mother, was second daughter of Malcom II, High King of Scotland before Duncan. She married the Mormaer of Moray, Findlaech MacRuaridh and Macbeth, whose name means 'Son of Life' was their only child, born in 1005.

During his early life, Macbeth would have been fostered out for his education, as was the ancient Celtic custom. Youths in powerful families learned a wide range of skills, covering traditional law, poetry, music, and of course warfare and individual skills in battle. Scotland did not maintain a regular army in the modern sense, but each great family had to provide bands of warriors, who in turn were individually responsible for their efforts to protect areas, or if needed, the entire realm.

Macbeth was elected to the High Kingship in August 1040 at Scone, the traditional king-making centre or sacred place of Scotland. Duncan, the previous ruler, had reigned for five years as High King. He had suffered five defeats in war, and his policy of aggression and expansion had proved disastrous for Scotland. When elected to the High Kingship, Macbeth was thirty-five years of age, mature and at the prime of life.

Macbeth grew up in a land that was partly Celtic and partly Norse. The large Norse territories in the far north and the islands of Orkney played an important role in the development of what was to later become Scotland. In the case of Macbeth and his eventual rulership, the Norse balance of power was crucial to success.

Generally, what we now know as Scotland was called Alba in the eleventh century, though the name Scotland (from *Scotti* or Irish skirmishers) was beginning to appear. Scotland and Ireland shared a common language, cultural heritage, and frequently employed each other's mercenaries for campaigns or sea defences. The overall picture is of a diffuse, constantly feuding collective of chieftains and rulers in both Scotland and Ireland, with a powerful Norse element ruling the far north and posing a constant threat to southern territories during the summer, sailing and raiding seasons.

While Alba, or Scotland, spoke a Celtic language, the Orkneys and Sutherland and Caithness primarily spoke Norse or a mixture of Norse/Celtic dialects due to intermarriage. The northern border of Alba was south of Sutherland and Caithness, but the southern border extended far into what is nowadays England . . . including Cumbria, and stretching approximately to the present border of Lancashire.

The six ancient provinces of Alba were established around the ninth century by union of the Picts and Scots – the Picts being the earliest inhabitants of the land, while the Scots were later incomers from Ireland. Over these territories, the *Ard Righ* or High King was elected to rule. It is significant, particularly in the context of the later vilification of Macbeth in literature, that this kingship was elective and not hereditary. This important difference of ruling system led to many later misunderstandings of the early politics of Scotland.

Before his election to the crown, Macbeth was involved in the hereditary power struggle between two of the largest provinces, Moray and Atholl. Macbeth's father ruled Moray, which was a large territory (larger than the modern Scottish county) stretching from the east coast of what is now Aberdeenshire to the west coast. This province was so powerful that chroniclers sometimes referred to the mormaers of Moray as 'Kings of Scotland', implying that its size and importance favoured the election of kings from among the mormaers.

The second largest province was Atholl in the west. The feuds between Atholl and Moray were often of a violent and bloody nature. Atholl included Scone, the king-making centre of Alba (in what is now Perthshire), and stretched westwards to the Western Isles, including Mull, Islay, Jura, Arran, and to the holy island of Iona. On Iona, kings were buried, and from Iona Christianity had spread to pagan Scotland by the efforts of the missionary saints under the guidance of St. Columba. It was from the mormaers of Atholl that High Kings of Alba were usually elected, because of their descent from earlier Irish (Dalriadic) rulers who had unified the west of the land.

Macbeth's Scotland: Eleventh Century

To understand the culture, the feuds, and the final fusion into a united kingdom for the first time under Macbeth, we need to examine briefly the way of life in tenth and eleventh century Scotland. Firstly, there were no large cities or towns: life was essentially rural and decentralised. The cultural basis was that of the family or clan, with much isolation and wilderness leading to

Silver jewellery from a Viking hoard buried in Skaill, Orkney. In Macbeth's time, Viking raids on the British coast were extensive.

9

fiercely independent people and territories. It was this independent strongly tribal background that developed into a system of elective leadership, and which did not favour hereditary kingship as it eventually developed in England and other parts of Europe. Cattle were the major source of wealth, livelihood, trade – and, of course, of theft and dispute. This style of life derived from the primal Celtic culture, represented best in the Irish epic of the *Cattle Raid of Cooley* and the adventures of Cuchulainn. But the people of the tenth and eleventh centuries were not tribal nomads; they had developed agriculture in the fertile regions, and had a strong reliance upon the sea, its trade routes, and upon fishing. It is clear that trade with mainland Europe was conducted by sea, and that many Irish and Scottish missionaries carried the word of the old Celtic Church to the east by such sea routes. In the period of Macbeth, however, there was a constant threat to sea travel and trade by the Norse or Viking marauders, particularly during the summer season which was the traditional (and essentially practical) period for raiding, sailing, and all forms of warfare on land or sea.

Settlements with any significance were centred upon two types of location; the ancient fortresses or *duns*, and the monastic centres. Although the original Celtic Church, predating the Roman Church, was not political or highly organised in the modern sense, monasteries had become centres of trade and industry by the eleventh century; this held true in some regions of Scotland, though not to as great an extent as in Europe.

Warriors – Scottish and Norman

In Macbeth's youth, there were constant threats from the North and South, with raiding Norsemen and Anglo-Saxons at either border region.

Scottish warriors of this period tended not to use body armour, or bows. This preference reminds us of the earliest records of the fighting Celts, who are described as charging naked into battle, inspired by a terrible frenzy. By the tenth and eleventh centuries, Scots were fighting with swords and small *targets* or round shields, covered with stiff leather. Chieftains' shields carried rich decorations, often used as means of identifying a leader during the confusion of a battle. The swords used by the Scots tended to be the long swords of enduring Celtic preference, with additional broad bladed daggers and spears.

Recreation was found through horse racing and hunting, particularly the deer hunt which originally held a sacred significance as well as the secular one of sport or food.

We might safely assume that the use of the fighting axe was common at least in the northern territories and western isles, where Norse settlers had mixed with the native Celtic population. The concept of the mailed and mounted warrior, soon to appear with the powerful Norman warriors, would not have been found in Scotland at the time of Macbeth's youth; but it almost certainly began to register in the south of Scotland during his reign, with the increasing Norman presence and interest in English territories.

The St. Ninian treasure from the Shetland Isles, including communion implements, an engraved bowl with animal motifs, an ornate sword pommel, a sword scabbard tip, a silver hanging bowl with a close detail showing the dog motif.

11

Viking warrior, from a tenth century carving.

Towards the close of his reign, Macbeth gave refuge to Norman warriors fleeing from retribution in England. These men were employed as mercenary troops to help defend the southern border; this action was possibly due to Macbeth's alliance with Thorfinn of Orkney and the potential balance of power both in England and Europe, though it is difficult to find evidence. The presence of Normans in Scotland, however, would have been seen as an ongoing threat to the English supremacy, and perhaps the beginning of an increased interest by Duke William of Normandy in the Scottish border territories as an access area into England. The Scottish and Celtic systems of government and elected kingship, together with the role of religion, were vital factors in Macbeth's rise to power.

Scottish Kingship

The old Scottish system of law, by which High Kings were elected and not drawn from hereditary lines as a matter of course, was a direct descendant of the oral traditions of law found in all early Celtic cultures. Late variants of these laws survived in Ireland, Wales and Brittany. They were the cause of much confusion to chroniclers and historians who failed to understand their foundation, assuming that the Scots were barbarians who flouted the general (English) laws of civilised existence. It was this system of elective kingship which made Macbeth into the first king of a progressive and increasingly united Scotland. Paradoxically, it also led to his unjustified vilification in later literature as an unscrupulous man of evil and so it is a system well worth examining.

Scotland was ruled by a complex of chieftains, ranging from small heads of

12

families, through to the mormaers or stewards, and culminating in lesser or petty kings directly under the High King. Significantly, all of these offices were well defined by ancient sets of laws, and all were maintained through election rather than inheritance. Candidates for power were nominated by their chieftain when death seemed imminent; such nominees were known as *tanists* (seconds). This system, so curious to the modern mind, seems to date back to a sacro-magical role of kingship common to primal western cultures. Elements of this pagan quality to kingship remained in eleventh century Scotland, which had a curious mixture of Christian and pre-Christian beliefs and practices.

Modern Scone, originally the sacred centre of Scotland where the Celtic kings were installed after their election.

The *tanist* or nominee needed tribal or clan approval to take his place as ruler. The greater leaders such as the mormaers or the High Kings were elected by a national assembly of chieftains and leaders of religion. There was a tendency for the great families to be elected to great roles; their experience in ruling and power led to a general pattern in which kingship was kept within certain family lines. But this was not identical to the English or European law of primogeniture, and there was no guaranteed succession.

It is this elective system that was so hard for later chroniclers to understand, and which led to the great drama of Shakespeare, which had little to do with the historical Macbeth. The principle behind elected kings was that they should be drawn from among those best suited and most worthy of the office . . . not merely from a family that sought to hold power. Petty chieftains and High Kings alike could be deposed by their people, and this acted as a guard against corruption or abuse of power.

Great families, such as Moray and Atholl, tended to be elected to the High

13

Kingship or other high office. In effect, this was a hereditary element within the elective system. The tendency for such families to feud with one another often led to attempts at deposing a High King through the ambition or vengeance of another chieftain or mormaer. In short, the system, which may have had its roots in a religious or magically-orientated society, had become politicised. With an ambitious series of invading kings ruling over nearby England, which developed an increasingly hereditary system, there were further options to abuse the Scottish system, by making alliances over the border. Such alliances were also made with Norway and Sweden.

Celtic Government

Despite the possibilities of abuse, the Celtic electoral system of rulership, from High King to local leader, worked well within the tolerances of its society and regions. It was supported and unified within a broader communal base of land tenure, from which the elected leadership system was derived. All land was held in common, there was no concept of private ownership or royal rights over tracts of land. The laws and restrictions of land and property administration were held in an ancient originally oral tradition. This began to become corrupted through the influence of the Roman Church, which was based upon a political system of ownership and manipulative legality, rather than tradition and consensus. Regional traditions of common ownership, labour and assistance remained in the remote parts of Scotland until the nineteenth century, so deep rooted were patterns of collective living.

Perhaps the most interesting aspect of Celtic traditional law, from the modern viewpoint, is the role of women. Unlike the legal situation which developed in England, and which persists in many aspects even today, marriage did not deprive a woman of her rights or her potential. Women were entitled to take elective office equally with men, and retained their personal powers, possessions and authority. This emphasis upon feminine equality and power derives from an earlier culture, best represented to us in the Irish sagas, in which women were direct representatives of the power or sovereignty of the goddess of the land. In this context, it is interesting to note that royal power (in England as well as Scotland) often depended upon the King marrying a certain woman. In the case of Macbeth, his marriage to Gruach, originally wife of his rival, confirmed his role of leadership. We should not take these primal magical aspects of early history too literally; they worked more in the manner of long established but vaguely defined sub-traditions. They occurred because they had always occurred, and because such processes as the relationship between a queen, the king, and land, were part of the deepest foundation of Celtic culture.

The Celtic Church

Religion played a crucial role at the time of Macbeth's life and his ascent to the throne of Alba or Scotland. The Celtic Church, one of the primal Christian churches predating the political Roman Church, came to Scotland

Celtic crozier found in Scandinavia and probably Viking loot from Scotland.

14

as early as 563 A.D. St Columba, banished from his native Ireland, established the first monastery on Iona, already a holy island with druidic pagan sanctity. Missionaries soon set to work to convert the Picts and Scots, and the Celtic Church was, loosely speaking, the state church of Scotland until at least the eleventh century. Even after the introduction of Roman monastic order through the reformation of the Saxon Queen Margaret (wife of Malcolm Canmore), there were still pockets of the Celtic or *culdee* orders surviving as late as the fourteenth century. Many Celtic church practices, fused with pagan tradition, survived well into the nineteenth and twentieth centuries in remote regions of the Highlands and islands, as communal prayers, rituals, and folklore.

The Celtic Church placed an emphasis upon communal living, non-ownership of land (in keeping with the traditional law of Celtic culture) and a diffusion of the Gospels in the common tongue (Gaelic or whatever happened to be the native language of a region). Great artists and scholars of Latin, Greek and Hebrew were found among the Celtic monks. It seems very likely that the education of the young Macbeth, son of a great mormaer, would have been at least partly under the guidance of the Celtic Church.

One of the important matters at the time of Macbeth's reign was the difference between the political land- and property-owning Roman Church, and the simpler more traditional Celtic Church. As an increasing tendency for

Scottish Christian relics: the Dunvegin Cup and the Kilmichael–Classrie Bell Shrine. The still active Celtic church in Scotland was supported by Macbeth.

15

the churches to own land developed, so did abbeys, settlements, crafts and trade centres become potential fortresses, targets for attack, and political weapons of bribery or corruption. Crinan, the father of Duncan, was both a warrior and an abbot. From his apparently ecclesiastical position at the Abbey of Dunkeld, Crinan was also Mormaer of Atholl and led an unsuccessful armed insurrection against Macbeth. This type of worldly exercise of power through a centre of religious authority was by no means typical of the Celtic Church, though many of its primates and saints were, of necessity, also warriors. Generally, the traditions and background of the Roman and Celtic Churches are very different. We may see the conflict between the older form of Christianity and its Roman political version as crucial to the emergence of a new and increasingly European Scotland. Similar conflicts were occuring all over Europe, where religion was used as an excuse to preserve or seize power.

The Rise to Power

Macbeth's rise to power and his final election to the High Kingship of Scotland thus took place against a complex political background. It also was closely interwoven with the fortunes and fates of other significant figures of the time.

Thorfinn of Orkney

Closely involved with Macbeth's rise to power was another important figure of the period. It would be no exaggeration to say that Thorfinn of Orkney was crucial to Macbeth's ascendance. Thorfinn descended from Malcolm II, who supported Thorfinn's claim to part of Orkney, and to the mainland territories of Caithness and Sutherland. To do this, Malcolm worked a vague dividing line between Celtic and Norse law, solely to obtain his own ends.

When Thorfinn's father, Sigurd Hlodversson, was slain at the great battle of Clontarf (1014) in Ireland, Orkney and the northern territories lay open to disputed claims. The defeat of the Norse invaders at the hand of the Irish was devastating; Norse expansion into Celtic regions was halted. Thus Malcolm's support of the young Thorfinn was designed to gradually claim back those territories taken from the Celts by force of arms. Thorfinn was sent to be fostered in the Norse–Celtic region of Caithness, ready to lay claim to a share of Orkney as soon as he was old enough.

Thus, to the north of Alba as ruled by Malcolm II, lay a large territory of both mainland and islands. Ultimately, these came under the rule of Thorfinn, who was sponsored by the Scottish king. It would not have been possible for Macbeth to come to the throne and develop Alba into a united kingdom, without some agreement with the powerful Thorfinn. Although we have no formal record of such an agreement, this is undoubtedly what must have occurred.

Known as the 'ruddy' or 'red-haired' king, Macbeth leads a raid upon rebels. In eleventh century Scotland, it was not unusual for a king to fight in person, taking the same risks as his warriors and thus ensuring his relationship as leader of his men.

However, Malcolm II did not rest with his inroads into the Norse territories through diplomacy and patronage. To the south, invading Danes and Saxons were battling for the rule of England, which fell to the great King Canute in 1016. Malcolm used the conflict to expand his own territories, invading the territory once known as Bernica on the east coast well into Northumbria. The Scots defeated the Northumbrians at Carham in 1018. Thus, the dispute for this territory between English and Danish overlords was turned to a decisive Scots advantage, and the rule of the High King was extended to its furthest point south.

Death of Macbeth's father

In the year 1020, when Macbeth was about fifteen years of age, his father Finlaech MacRuaridh was slain by his nephews Gillecomgain and Malcolm. The killing probably took place because of Finlaech's increasing connections with the rival House of Atholl. He had married King Malcolm II's daughter Doada, and given support to the High King by placing his clans under royal command during Danish raids. Thus, whilst no definite reason is known, we may presume that the ongoing feud between Moray and Atholl led to the killing. The nephew Malcolm was elected as Mormaer, and died after nine years of rule; Gillecomgain was immediately elected to rule after his brother.

Unlike his uncle Gillecomgain stood firmly against the Atholl High King. He sought to improve the Moray claim to High Kingship by marrying Gruach, who was later to become the wife of Macbeth. Gruach was the granddaughter of Kenneth III, who had been killed by Malcolm II in 1005.

This pattern of dispute, election, and symbolic defiance through marriage, is crucial to the eventual kingship of Macbeth.

Death of Gillecomgain

History tells us little of what happened to Macbeth after the death of his father. Presumably he was under the protection of Malcolm II, and grew into adulthood in some safe place, receiving his training in arms and skill as befitted a member of a noble family who had supported the High King. In 1032, according to the *Annals of Ulster*, the Mormaer of Moray and fifty of his men were burned to death. Gillecomgain, cousin to Macbeth and killer of Macbeth's father, had finally fallen victim in turn to the Moray and Atholl feud. During Malcolm's old age, pressure had been building over the High Kingship and his nominated successor; a number of battles and killings were a direct result of this tension, as the election of a new High King was imminent. Thus, Malcolm II, at the age of almost eighty, sought to eliminate as many possible candidates for the High Kingship as he could in the limited time left to him. Gillecomgain's marriage to Gruach, his powerful Moray position, and his obvious hostility to Atholl, brought about his death. His son Lulach and Gruach, however, escaped the slaughter, though in 1033 her brother (another Malcolm) was killed in the ruthless process of eliminating opposition to the Atholl claim and to the nominee of the aged king.

The fearsome Earl Siward, leader of the English expedition against Scotland and Macbeth, prepares to leap to his death from the walls of York. Stricken by camp fever or dysentery, he demanded to be dressed in full armour and carried outdoors, rather than die inside like an animal on straw.

Glamis Castle, despite its legendary claims, has little real historical association with Macbeth.

Mormaer of Moray

In 1033, Macbeth was elected as Mormaer of Moray. There is much debate over the part he may or may not have played in the killing of Gillecomgain, the slayer of his father. Certainly, the deaths of Gillecomgain and Malcolm Mac Bodhe (brother of Gruach) were part of the Atholl plan to retain power by wiping out all potential candidates for High King from the Moray faction. But there is no contemporary evidence to suggest that Macbeth was directly involved.

It seems unlikely that Macbeth was a direct puppet of Malcolm II, otherwise he would not have been elected as Mormaer. Whatever the reasons for his election, he soon married Gruach (the widow of Gillecomgain and granddaughter of a Scottish king) and adopted her son Lulach. Thus, on coming into his territorial power, he took on the traditional stance of opposition to the House of Atholl. Suddenly, Macbeth had become one of the most powerful men in Alba, with a strong claim as potential candidate for the High Kingship. Curiously, the ageing Malcolm II had not removed Macbeth from the scene, though we have no evidence to support or deny any such attempts.

Duncan becomes High King

Malcolm finally died at Glamis, on November 25th in 1034. His nominated successor was Duncan Mac Crinan, his eldest grandson, who was elected as High King at Scone in December 1034. Thus does one of the most bitter conflicts for power related in dramatic literature make its *true* historical appearance.

Duncan was thirty three years old, and had some experience of rule as petty king of Cumbria. His election seemed to place the House of Atholl firmly in the highest role of power in Alba.

After the death of King Canute in 1035, and the subsequent struggles of the English and Norwegian crowns, Thorfinn became ruler of the entire Orkneys, Hebrides, and the mainland regions of Caithness and Sutherland. The rise of Thorfinn is only of interest in as much as it affected the career of Macbeth, but by 1039–40, two grandsons of Malcolm II ruled Scotland from north to south: Thorfinn, the old king's Norse protegé, and Duncan his elected heir to the High Kingship of Alba. This two-fold division of power finally brought Macbeth to the throne, but not without the catalysing effect of Duncan's inability to rule adequately.

Macbeth was, of course, another grandson of Malcolm II through his mother Doada. Thus, the cautious policy of marrying a daughter, Doada, into the opposing Moray faction to gain support would soon turn against the House of Atholl.

Duncan Overthrown

MACDUFF   O horror, horror, horror! Tongue nor heart Cannot conceive or name thee.

MACBETH & LENNOX   What's the matter?

MACDUFF   Confusion now hath made his masterpiece. Most sacrilegious murder hath broke ope The Lord's anointed temple, and stole thence the life o' th' building

MACBETH   What is't you say – the life?

LENNOX   Mean you his majesty?

MACDUFF   Approach the chamber and destroy your sight With a new Gorgon. Do not bid me speak; see and then speak yourselves. Awake! Awake! Ring the alarum bell. Murder and treason! . . .

In Shakespeare's drama, Duncan is described as a gracious king, slain by a foul usurper. The historical truth, well attested, is rather the opposite. When Duncan was deposed, no complaint was raised, and Macbeth was *elected*. This matter of election is not entirely proof of universal approval, but goes a long way towards proving that Macbeth was a better choice for the people of Alba than was the late Duncan.

In *The Orygynale Cronykil of Scotland*, Andrew Wyntoun describes Duncan as a vicious tyrant; certainly his record as a ruler and military leader is poor. The fictional warping of history, by which the roles of Macbeth and Duncan were gradually reversed, did not begin until some centuries after the original events; by which point time and cultural changes had obscured the reality of the situation.

Perhaps Duncan's most unpopular and dangerous move was to force campaigns on northern and southern fronts almost simultaneously. Duncan

attempted to expand into the territories of Caithness and Sutherland, ruled by the powerful earl Thorfinn of Orkney as part of the Norse territories. He also tried to take advantage of the disputes over English succession, by invading Northumbria. Thus, forces moved both north and south, to Caithness under the command of Duncan's nephew Moddan, and to Durham under the command of Duncan himself. Both attempts failed miserably.

Duncan, showing himself not only to be heartless but totally incapable of basic military strategy, sent repeated cavalry charges against the massive walls of Durham; once the cavalry were defeated, the city troops counter-attacked and killed thousands of the Scottish infantry. The heads of these men, killed through the incompetence of the king that they had helped to elect, were impaled around the city walls.

While in retreat, Duncan met with his nephew Moddan, who had been forced to withdraw from Caithness and Sutherland in the face of a large opposing force assembled by Thorfinn and his foster father Thorkell. Duncan then resolved to throw all his remaining combined forces against Thorfinn, with a land army commanded by Moddan, and Duncan heading a fleet of eleven ships to attempt to trap the Norse warriors in between two attacking armies.

Ornamental sword hilts (above and opposite) by the Frankish swordsmiths who produced the best weapons of the period, and which were widely used throughout Europe and Northern Scotland.

Defeat at Sea

Earl Thorfinn met Duncan's fleet off Deerness, where after a prolonged sea battle, the Scottish ships were routed. Much of the history of this period is recorded in the *Orkneyinga Saga* which describes the battle between the Orkney and Scottish fleets in detail:

The Scots bunched together on the High King's ship just before the mast. Then Jarl Thorfinn leaped from the poop of his ship forward into that of the High King, laying about him boldly. When he saw that the numbers were thinning upon the High King's ship, he called on his men to come aboard. And when King Duncan saw this, he gave orders to cut the lashing and stand off to sea . . .

Duncan escaped from his doomed flagship to another vessel, and headed south. Thorfinn combined his forces with another fleet led by his foster father Thorkell, and pursed the High King into the Moray Firth: Duncan made his way ashore, and the two Orkney fleets attacked the coastal settlements of the region.

Meanwhile Moddan and his force of Atholl clansmen had reached Caithness, where they awaited reinforcements of Irish mercenaries. Thorkell and his men, however, surprised Moddan's unfortunate troop while they slept. As Moddan leaped from a burning building, Thorkell beheaded him with a single blow. Duncan now assembled as large an army as possible and confronted Thorfinn on 14 August 1040, only to be defeated.

It is at this point in the tale that Macbeth again appears. The *Orkneyinga Saga* tells us that Duncan fled the battle 'and some say he was slain'.

Marianus Scotus, however, says that 'Duncan High King of Scotland was slain on 14 August by his general Macbeth, son of Finlay' (*Chronicon Univer-*

sal). This seems unlikely, given the circumstances of the feud between Atholl and Moray, unless some unchronicled duplicity was practised by Macbeth. No further evidence of this curious incident is now available, and we might assume from subsequent events that Macbeth was on good terms with Thorfinn of Orkney, without whose support he could not have remained as High King for fifteen years.

It seems more likely that we are dealing here with a clerical or copying error, and that Macbeth and his Moray forces helped to dispose of Duncan after the High King's failure against the Orkney men. One possible interpretation of this statement is that the Celtic title mormaer or something similar has been translated to mean 'general' by Marianus Scotus.

After the defeat and death of Duncan, who had become widely unpopular as a result of his expansionism and inability to rule or command adequately, events suggest an alliance between Thorfinn of Orkney and Macbeth Mormaer of Moray. The result was that Thorfinn was firmly established without any opposition or Scottish claims upon Orkney or Caithness and Sutherland, while Macbeth was elected to the High Kingship.

Duncan was actually killed at Bothgowan which means 'the blacksmith's house'; today the name has become Pitgaveny, near Elgin.

Contemporary reports vary slightly, for John of Fordun says that Duncan was wounded and carried to Elgin where he died; the *Register of St. Andrews* states that he died at Bothgowan. The Orkney forces ravaged far south into Fife, burning, killing, and destroying. We may presume that it was during this period that some arrangement was made between Thorfinn and Macbeth, for the Orkney forces eventually withdrew northwards. Macbeth made his way to Scone, the hallowed place of king making, to claim support and election as High King. He was crowned in the summer of 1040.

Macbeth as King

During his rule, Macbeth gave much to Scotland. Contemporary chronicles described him as liberal, and his reign as productive, plentiful, generous. St. Berchan, referring to the aftermath of the conflict between Duncan and Thorfinn wrote:

After the slaughter of the Scots, after the slaughter of foreigners, the liberal king will possess Scotland. This strong one was fair, yellow haired, tall. Very pleasant was that handsome youth to me. Brimful of food was Scotland, east and west, during the reign of the brave ruddy king.

How different is this account from that given by Shakespeare, hundreds of years later and as spoken by Macduff:

Fit to govern! No, not to live! O nation miserable with an untitled tyrant bloody-sceptred, when shalt thou see thy wholesome days again. . .

The Early Reign

From 1040 to 1045, the Kingdom of Alba was relatively peaceful, with the newly elected High King rebuilding after the ravages of Duncan's unsuccessful campaigns. Contemporary and later chroniclers generally confirm that Macbeth and his wife were good rulers. The tyrannical despotic element simply does not appear in the early sources of his history, those very sources which by their nature of closeness to the man and his rule are probably the most accurate.

Hector Boece, writing much later, in the early part of the sixteenth century, suggests that Macbeth became cruel and oppressive after 1050. Prior to that, Boece admits that the King initiated certain legal reforms (*History of Scotland*, 1527).

These reforms are interesting for they include statutory support of orphans and women, inheritance for daughters, and control over itinerant and non-productive members of the population for the benefit of the community. Laws of this sort are typical to the ancient oral traditions of law preserved in Celtic countries. They certainly would not have been novel or unusual in eleventh century Scotland which already upheld an exceedingly complex set of laws providing for women, common welfare, state support for the less fortunate, and as described earlier an archaic but operative system of common ownership and election of leaders, be they male or female.

Boece, much like Shakespeare copying from the histories without fully understanding their background, would not necessarily have grasped the cultural foundation for those laws which he ascribed generously to Macbeth. It is likely, though, that in the period of reform following his election, the new King declared formally that he would uphold certain essential laws deriving from ancient tradition – particularly if they were those that had fallen into disuse during the reign of the previous King.

We may also consider sources more contemporary for evidence of Macbeth's government of Alba in those early years; both the king and his wife Gruach were benefactors of the Celtic Church. They are recorded (in the *Register of St. Andrews*) as giving land to the Culdees of Loch Leven. Andrew Wyntoun also records, some centuries later, that Macbeth 'did many pleasant acts in the beginning of his reign . . .'

Thorfinn Invades the South

But the early years of the reign were not totally peaceful, and two invasions or series of raids occurred into England which shed some further light on the relationship between Macbeth and Earl Thorfinn of Orkney.

In 1041, Thorfinn established a base camp as far south as Strathclyde, from which he indulged in raids over the border into Northumbria. Earl Siward rooted out these invaders, and forced them to retreat. Thorfinn returned to Orkney, but raised a large army for the following spring of 1042.

The *Orkneyinga Saga* tells us that for this retaliatory expedition troops were drawn not only from Orkney and Caithness, but from Ireland and

Viking swords and axe head (above and opposite); typical weapons of the Macbeth period.

Scotland. The presence of Scottish troops indicates that Macbeth was somehow in allegiance with Thorfinn, even if it was only to the extent of allowing warriors to hire as mercenaries to the Norse Earl. Yet there was no official or formal declaration of war between Scotland and Northumbria, nor was Macbeth on record as a defined or formal ally of Thorfinn. This nebulous situation must have suited Macbeth well; he could keep the general support of the powerful Earl who had allowed him to stand for the Scottish throne, yet avoid a total declaration of hostilities that might spill over into war with England.

Thorfinn's fleet struck at Cumbria on the north western coast of England, and defeated the Mercians there in two battles before the onset of winter. (We must remember that the campaigning season was fairly short, and that all wars were punctuated by the need to return homewards before winter; this was a vital feature of all medieval warfare and seasonal and weather factors were often decisive in the outcome of campaigns.) The conflict was nobly recorded by Arnor, the *skald* or bard to Earl Thorfinn as the following extract shows:

> Upon England's shores
> The Jarl bore his banner
> Ever and again.
> Reddening the Eagle's tongue,
> The Prince bade them carry
> The Standard steadfastly.
> Flame flared,
> Roofs fell, smoke curled,
> To heaven rose the fiery gleam
> While the armed band pursued.
>
> Many horn blast
> Was heard 'mid the fortresses
> Where high wind waved the banner
> Of the stout hearted Prince.
> He of the open hand,
> Rushed into battle.
> Now fear fell
> On the Wolf Lord's host.
> In the battle at dawn
> Swords were washed
> And wolves tore the slain. . . .

The Revolt of Crinan

Contemporary chronicles record that in 1045, Crinan, father of Duncan and Abbot of Dunkeld, was killed with 180 of his Atholl men. This was the only internal revolt of any significance that occurred during Macbeth's reign. The campaigns that eventually destroyed him were backed by troops from Northumbria, England, or Denmark. Obviously, Crinan judged that after five years of Moray-sponsored rule, the time was ripe for an Atholl revolt. His forces met with those of Macbeth at Dunkeld, north of Perth. Both the Mormaer of Atholl and his men were killed, and no further Atholl insurrec-

Modern Dunkeld, which in Macbeth's time was the seat of power of Crinan, the warrior abbot and father of Duncan.

tion occurred for some years until the invasions in support of Malcolm, by then exiled at the English court.

After Crinan's revolt and death, nine years of increasing stability occurred in Scotland. Macbeth made the traditional monarch's pilgrimage to Rome to obtain absolution from the Pope – and of course to confirm and connect his political sources of support within Europe and the Church of Rome which claimed a general overlordship of all kings, states, and variant Churches.

Peace and Prosperity

It seems that Macbeth's years of peace and prosperity were due in a great measure to the strength of Earl Thorfinn. Shortly after the Atholl revolt and the death of Crinan, Thorfinn came into conflict with his nephew Rognvald Brussisson, who disputed the division of Orkney. As this dispute matured, Rognvald had the support of King Magnus of Norway, and for a while the prospects looked hard indeed for Thorfinn, and were thus threatening to Macbeth. If Rognvald defeated Thorfinn with the aid of Magnus, then a renewed powerful Norwegian claim upon Orkney, Caithness and Sutherland would soon follow.

Despite warships supplied by Norway to aid his cause, Rognvald was defeated in a terrible sea battle in the Pentland Firth. He fled to the court of

King Magnus, but almost immediately returned to make a desperate assassination attempt upon the unsuspecting Thorfinn. The *Orkneyinga Saga* relates how Rognvald and his men set fire to the hall in which Thorfinn sat drinking, and how it was assumed that Thorfinn and his wife Ingibjorg had died in the conflagration. But Thorfinn had carried his wife to safety, breaking through the back wall of the hall, and had rowed to Caithness.

In secrecy, Thorfinn took reports of Rognvald's movements, and finally trapped him upon the island of Stronsay. Rognvald's attempt to escape was foiled by his own lapdog, which barked and gave away his position. The usurping nephew was killed by Thorkell, foster father to Thorfinn.

If Magnus of Norway had been able at this stage to invade in force, using the death of his man Rognvald as an excuse, Orkney might have fallen. But Magnus was soon embroiled in conflict over the rulership of Denmark. This was claimed both by Magnus and by the regent Sweyn after the death of Hardecanute, who had been king of both England and, at one remove, of Denmark. Thus, Thorfinn was able to assert his independence from Norway, and provide alliance and protection for Alba from his position of strength in the far north.

Edward the Confessor, crowned in 1043, now ruled England. The crown and its connection to Europe was the subject of complex feuds and disputes. This situation enabled Alba and its king Macbeth to remain in comparative isolation and freedom from invasion. Paradoxically, it was this same complex political situation that nurtured Malcolm Canmore, son of Duncan. He absorbed the concept, hitherto hardly recognised in Alba, that there was a hereditary right of kingship passing from father to eldest son. This is where the deepest roots of the concept of Macbeth as a usurper may be tentatively traced; roots which were to sprout in chronicles and histories several centuries after the death of Macbeth, and to flower in Shakespearian drama and derivative works of art.

Invasion, Downfall and Death

The turning point in Macbeth's period of generous and unifying rule was 1054. Malcolm, son of Duncan, gained support from the English king Edward for his claim the High Kingship of Alba. Such a claim was inadmissible under Celtic law; but it was certainly admissible in England, where primogeniture carried considerable weight. Overall command for an invasion force was given to Earl Siward of Northumbria.

Siward was a truly heroic character, large in size and nature, to whom many exploits were traditionally attributed. His significant service to Edward the Confessor was to cut off the head of a rebellious earl (Jarl Tosti) and deliver it to the King. In July of 1054, Siward Dirga (Valiant) led a large army of his own Northumbrians, plus Danes and Anglo-Saxons, over the border into Scotland. The *Anglo Saxon Chronicle* records that he slaughtered many

Scots, and that Macbeth was put to flight. Siward lost his own son in this conflict, and so the war became not only a matter of political expansionism, but one of personal revenge. Malcolm accompanied the invading forces, raising Atholl supporters to his cause.

The primary objective of the invading army was Scone, centre of king-making. Presumably Malcolm hoped to accumulate enough support to be elected or declared king as soon as Macbeth had been disposed of. The battle listed in the chronicles is of course the famous scene in Shakespeare's play in which 'Birnam wood do come to Dunsinane'.

Despite the curious tradition found in Shakespeare, we can also trace this motif to the thirteenth century prophecies of Thomas the Rhymer, who predicted that 'Fedderate Castle shall ne'er be ta'en/till Fyvie wood to the war is gaen . . .'

This utterance was dramatically fulfilled in the eighteenth century, when invading English troops used trees from Fyvie wood as battering rams to breach the previously unconquered castle of Feddarate. It is impossible to tell where Shakespeare drew his tradition from; did the wood motif come from an actual tradition relating to the eleventh century and Macbeth, later adapted by Thomas the Rhymer into a coincidentally accurate prophetic verse? Or did Shakespeare – as seems more likely – draw the theme from his own reading of the popular verses and *Romance* of Thomas the Rhymer?

The siting of the battle at Dunsinane seems likely, but is not confirmed by contemporary chroniclers. Dunsinane lies between Scone and Perth, so it is certainly in the correct region. William of Malmesbury, writing in the twelfth century, suggests that the conflict took place at Dundee. Once again, there is no body of supporting evidence from the period.

The battle was not decisive with losses of 3,000 Scots, and 1,500 English and Danes. Siward lost his son, Oshern, and was forced to withdraw without placing Malcolm upon the throne, and without killing Macbeth. He also lost his nephew, another Siward; the price he paid for his invasion was high.

Malcolm was officially recognised as King of Cumbria, confirmed by Edward the Confessor, and thus described in a letter from the English court to Pope Boniface. But he was not yet King of Scotland. As an added setback to his ambitions, Earl Siward died in York the following year – not in battle, but of some type of illness, possibly dysentery. Before his death, he ordered that he should be attired in full battle array with armour, shield and axe: 'I will not die like a cow on straw . . . ' Tradition preserves the tale of his dramatic death leap from the city walls rather than die on his sick bed.

The Earldom of Northumbria was now taken over by Edward's favourite Tostig Godwinson. Two years elapsed in which Tostig, a firm comrade of Malcolm, supported plans for renewed invasion of Scotland.

Viking swords from the ninth and tenth century: single edged (above); double-edged and five-lobed pommelled, double-edged (opposite).

The Death of Macbeth

Ultimately, Macbeth's end was inexorably linked with the subsequent history of Duncan's family.

26

The immediate relatives of Duncan had not been wiped out by Macbeth, nor had any immediate plan of revenge been exacted upon them. Duncan's father Crinan, the Abbot of Dunkeld, had been a renowned warrior in his day. He made arrangements for his three grandsons to be fostered outside the immediate circle of the court of Alba, not only for their immediate protection, but to train them as potential candidates for the High Kingship.

The eldest of these boys was Malcolm, aged nine. His mother was cousin to Siward, who became Earl of Northumbria in 1041. This relationship was to prove crucial to Macbeth. Both son and mother were sent to the English court, where they lived through the short violent reign of Hardecanute, into that of Edward the Confessor.

The young Malcolm thus learned English ways rather than Celtic, speaking the various languages of the different factions. These included Norman French, which was already spoken at court before the Norman Conquest as a result of Edward's own exile in Normandy before he became king. Malcolm's period in England can be viewed as the beginning of the end for the old style elected High Kingship, for when he took the throne from Macbeth some years later, he brought many European ways into Celtic Scotland, accelerating changes already begun.

The second son of Duncan MacCrinan was Donald Ban, aged seven at the time of his exile. He was fostered either in the Hebrides or in Ireland, thus retaining Celtic customs of education and culture. This native upbringing was to show when he, in turn, became High King after his brother Malcolm.

The third son, Maelmuir, was sent to the court of his relative Siward of Northumbria; he eventually succeeded his grandfather as Mormaer of Atholl.

Thus, three potential claimants to the throne were fostered in three diverse areas, and at least two were in camps directly hostile to Macbeth: Malcolm in England, and Maelmuir in Northumbria. We may presume that Donald Ban was hidden right in the midst of staunch Atholl supporters in the west of Scotland or in Ireland, to be trained for the enduring conflict between his House and that of Moray represented by Macbeth. On confirmation as king of Cumbria, supported by the English crown, Malcolm continued to work towards his goal; the High Kingship of Scotland, and of course the death of Macbeth. Traditionally, Malcolm would have had support from the Atholl clans, but it is not clear who succeeded Crinan as mormaer after his death in 1045. After the invasion of 1054, Macbeth retained control of much of Scotland, including Scone, the traditional seat of power.

The lengthy process of destroying Macbeth, over a period of at least three years, suggests that his good qualities of rule, as recorded by early chronicles, had gained him widespread support. He was by no means easy to dispose of, but history and the tides of change in Europe now worked against him. His visit to Rome for absolution by Leo IX was now rendered valueless as a political connection; Leo died in 1054 as a prisoner in the ongoing feud with the invading Normans in Italy. The firm support for Malcolm from Edward, and from his vassal Tostig, could not be countered with appeals to papal

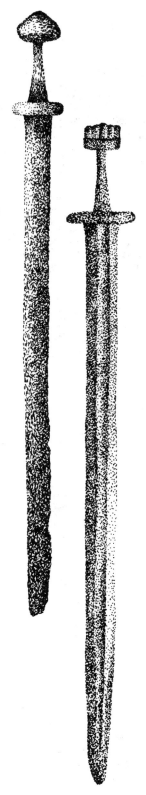

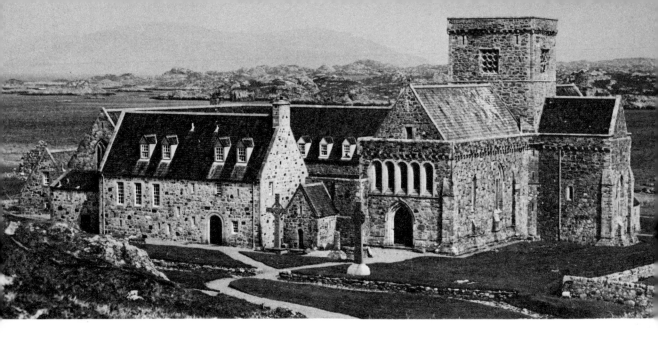

Iona Abbey on the sacred island of Iona was the traditional burial place of Scottish kings and nobles and where Macbeth and his wife Gruach were laid.

authority. Furthermore, Macbeth had given refuge to a number of Normans banished from England during the struggles for power; these warriors were almost all killed during the great battle of 1054. The sheltering and use of Norman mercenaries, however, was seen as a direct threat to English power, as Scotland might become a base from which the ambitious Duke William of Normandy might eventually press his claims or attacks upon England.

In 1057, on 15th August, Malcolm killed Macbeth. Traditionally, this occurred in or near an ancient circle of stones called Peel Ring, at Lumphanan in Mar. Malcolm and his troops had pursued Macbeth northwards from Scone. Little is known of the reasons for this movement other than the presumed fact that the invading Anglo–Danish army had gradually weakened the southernmost defences and gained support from the Atholl faction – to such an extent that it became imperative for Macbeth to move his court and take a fresh stand in safer territory.

Macbeth was buried on the island of Iona, the sacred place where so many Scottish kings were traditionally interred. This honourable and venerable custom reveals once again that he was regarded as a just and rightful king. In contrast, Malcolm was buried in Dunfermline upon his death. This must reflect that he was not considered as worthy as his predecessors of the ancient burial right upon Iona, an island shrouded in mystery and traditions of sanctity.

The curious aspect of Macbeth's death in the stone circle may be worth further consideration. Just as we have the relics of an early culture in the theme of certain women remarrying the kings, mormaers or clan leaders in succession (as did Gruach, Macbeth's wife), so we may have a similar con-fused echo in the story of Macbeth's death. So many traditions are attached to kingship and ritual death in Celtic culture that it is hard not to find an over-tone of such traditions in the fact that Malcolm imposed a 'cruel death' upon the High King in a stone circle.

28

The Short Reign of Lulach

Scotland did not pass into the rulership of Malcolm immediately upon his killing of Macbeth. The invading troops presumably retired or were forced to retire southwards again, for Macbeth was carried with ceremony to Iona. His stepson Lulach, appointed as his *tanist* or potential successor, was elected as High King.

Lulach was elected at Scone in the manner of Celtic law, which clearly indicates that Malcolm was by no means popular or powerful enough at this stage, even after the death of Macbeth. But sheer weight of numbers, English support, and the weakening of Scotland through a long series of campaigns and destruction, were beginning to have their inevitable effect. Lulach resisted Malcolm's forces for seven months. A contemporary chronicle records that he was slain on 17th March, 1058, by treachery. Lulach was, in turn, to follow Macbeth for burial upon Iona, as was his mother Gruach. Their graves were to remain in the tiny burial ground next to the abbey for at least eight hundred years; today the burial stones have been moved for preservation.

King Malcolm

Thus on 25th April, 1058, Malcolm was finally crowned as High King by Bishop Tuthald, in Scone. It is interesting to realise that during this long campaign and the gradual suppression of the Moray House (which was to persist during Malcolm's reign with his oppression and eventual banishment of Lulach's son Mael Snechta) that no aid was forthcoming from Thorfinn of Orkney.

By 1059, or thereabouts, Thorfinn had died. In 1059, Malcolm married his widow, Ingibjorg – yet another example of a male ruler's power being confirmed through his marriage to the right woman. It seems likely that Thorfinn died of an illness, and was thus unable to lead direct support for Macbeth. He was one of the greatest of all Orkney rulers and widely lamented by Norse saga makers or chroniclers. The ruins of his great hall and his abbey on Birsay may still be found today.

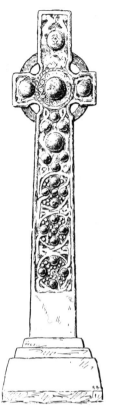

St. Martins Cross on the island of Iona.

The Kings of Scotland, including Macbeth, in the nineteenth century frieze in the Natural Portrait Gallery of Scotland, Edinburgh.

Thorfinn was the greatest warrior. He took the earldom when he was five winters old [ie supported in his claim by Malcom II] and he ruled for more than sixty winters; he died of disease in the latter days of Harald Sigurd's son.   *The Heimskringla of St. Olaf's Saga.*

The coincidence of dates of death between Macbeth and Thorfinn has caused some writers to suggest that Thorfinn died while campaigning in support of his Scottish ally; but there is no contemporary evidence to support this. Indeed, Norse sources state that he died of disease. The curious fact that Malcom Mac Duncan, now King Malcolm III, married Thorfinn's widow has added to the puzzle of this complex situation. Dorothy Dunnet, in her epic novel *King Hereafter* has gone so far as to suggest that Thorfinn and Macbeth were one and the same person, also conflating Gruach and Ingibjorg. The physical descriptions of the two men, however, would alone counter such a theory; Thorfinn described as tall grim and dark, while Macbeth was ruddy or golden in colouring.

Historical Legacy

During the seventeen years of Macbeth's reign, there were the first indications of a unified Scotland. This must not be taken in a literal sense, and much of the concept and process of unification may only be seen with hindsight. What is certain is that his murder and the eventual acquisition of the crown by Malcolm marked a turning point in the decline of ancient Scotland. It led to the gradual but almost total anglicising of the country and its methods of government. Once again, this hinges upon the matter of primogeniture, in which an eldest son has a firm right to his father's property or crown. Once this concept was introduced by force into the foundation of the Scottish Celtic system, it was inevitable that profound changes would follow.

This sequence of changes brought Scotland into step with the rapidly altering political consciousness of Europe. There would have been no likelihood of an idealised Alba or Scotland preserving Celtic communal traditions while all countries around were falling to the swords of the mighty and devising complex systems of preserving selected superior groups in power. Macbeth's reign was a lull in the storm of change, created by the balance of power between himself and Thorfinn of Orkney, and coincidentally assisted by the rapidly changing power struggles in England and Europe.

With Malcolm Canmore's claiming of the Scottish crown, feudalism came into the land, and there it remained. He gave large areas of land to his supporters, particularly in the Moray regions which would otherwise have opposed him. This granting of land as a possession to overlords was in itself essentially alien to the Scottish or Celtic system. It was much more than a move to weaken opposition, for it struck directly at the cultural roots of the people.

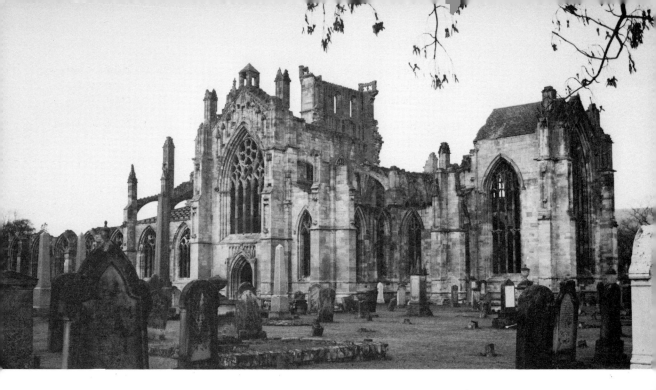

The dramatic events of the year 1066, by which William of Normandy forced his way upon the English throne, drove Edgar Aetheling, the English heir and only survivor of his family, into Scotland. As he had grown up in Hungary, Edgar could not speak English, and was not held in any esteem by the English nobles. Of course, the succession became irrelevant after the battles of 1066, but Edgar was given refuge by Malcolm. After the death of Ingibjorg during childbirth, Malcolm married Edgar's sister Margaret.

This marriage helped to hasten the decline of Scotland as a culture separate from Europe. Margaret was a supporter of the Roman Church, and made considerable efforts to Romanise the older primal Celtic Church, which had always kept itself separate from its younger and much more politically conscious relative in Rome. The most effective of her reforms was to place her Saxon confessor, Turgot, in the position of primate of Scotland. Although various *culdee* or Celtic practices were to remain for long periods of time, the formal status of the Celtic Church as the national spiritual organisation for the Scots was effectively destroyed by Margaret. She was, of course, canonized for her services, and Turgot wrote her biography.

But Margaret's formidable influence was not confined to religion; she controlled Malcolm. This control, leading to four invasions of England in support of her brother Edgar's claim to the English throne, also helped to weaken Scottish independance. After much bloodshed along the borders and in Northumbria, William the Conqueror finally invaded Scotland in retaliation. Malcolm submitted to William in 1072, at Abernethy, and swore to accept him as overlord.

However, the conflict between England and Scotland was not settled. By 1079 Malcolm was engaged in further hostilities over the border. After the

Melrose Abbey, one of the great border abbeys of Scotland. Such centres represented the 'new style' monarchy in Scotland after the death of Macbeth, when election of kings ceased.

death of William in 1087, his son William Rufus invaded Cumbria, which he took as part of England, and which it has remained to the present day. Malcolm failed to come to terms with William Rufus, and was finally killed during another invasion of Northumbria in 1093.

Upon the death of Malcolm (and that of his wife Margaret which followed shortly afterwards), his brother Donald Ban, now aged sixty, was elected High King at Scone. His brief reversion to Celtic style rule was soon wiped out by an invading army sponsored by England. This invasion was designed to set Duncan, son of Malcolm and previously hostage at the English court, upon the throne of Scotland. Duncan declared himself King by hereditary right, a declaration impossible under Scottish law.

Duncan was to rule for only a few months, and was killed by a supporter of Donald Ban, who returned to rule (as elected High King) for a further three years, until 1097. His reign was cruelly terminated by Edgar, yet another son of Malcolm and Margaret, supported once again by William Rufus and an invading army. Donald Ban was taken prisoner and blinded. Although he was buried at Dunkeld, his body was later taken to Iona as a sign of respect for a High King. Significantly, both Malcolm and Margaret remained buried in Dunfermline and were not accorded this honour.

Edgar, son of Malcolm, again declared a hereditary right to the crown, and the course was set for an Anglo–Norman ruling class in Scotland. From feuding between the Moray and Atholl factions, the struggle for the Scottish crown had finally become a matter of international politics, with a foreign power supporting rival claimants within one ruling faction. It seems ironic that this bitter true story of blood relatives fighting and killing one another should have been passed over, while the true history of Macbeth as a good king who benefitted his realm has been forgotten.

Shakespeare's Characters – and History

A comparison of the characters as portrayed by Shakespeare and their historical likelihood is illuminating. Not only do the historical persons bear very little relationship to those assembled by Shakespeare (who drew entirely upon relatively late chronicles), but we find that some of the major figures are the opposite of their fictional namesakes. This is most apparent in Macbeth himself, and in his opposite, Duncan.

While the historical Macbeth was a king of good character, Duncan was a tyrant. Lady Macbeth, Gruach, seems also to have been a person of good character and a beneficial queen; many of the ruthless qualities exhibited by the Shakespearian lady are more noticeable in Margaret, English wife of Malcolm III who invaded Scotland and killed Macbeth.

We need, however, to exercise a certain amount of caution when making such brief comparisons, particularly at such a long historical remove and through the filters of many literary sources. While it is easy to compare persons through such diffuse hindsight, the opposites and similarities are really little more than the natural rhythmn that arises in any historical period.

Norse raiders from Orkney attack an isolated southern Scottish settlement. Despite support for Macbeth from the powerful Earl Thorfinn of Orkney, there were still raids around the southern Scottish coasts.

In other words, when we examine the chronicles of kings, queens and people of power, some few are of good character, while many more are ruthless and devious. Furthermore, the standard of judgement is coloured by time and cultural change. Macbeth was a relatively good kind by any standard, less bloodthirsty and destructive by far than his immediate predecessor Duncan; yet he undoubtedly killed and manipulated his supporters, as did any leader of the period. Within a few years Malcolm, son of Duncan, was already colouring Macbeth as a usurper, a theme that was to be developed so readily in centuries to come. Thus, from the viewpoint of the hereditary monarch, Macbeth and the system which he upheld of elected leadership, were evils that threatened the hard won status quo of armed power and primogeniture. Some of the people in the list which follows *do* appear on the surface to be inversions or confusions of one another. Yet there is no evidence whatsoever that this is anything other than coincidence and the organic change of characters that runs through history. Shakespeare and his chronicle sources did *not* confuse these characters with one another.

Sir Laurence Olivier plays Macbeth in Shakespeare's play.

MACBETH   Presented by Shakespeare as a usurper, tyrant, and murderer. But history shows that he was an elected king with seventeen years of general support and beneficial rule to his credit.

LADY MACBETH   Portrayed as a powerful influence upon the corrupt acts of the tyrant Macbeth; a ruthless woman bent upon revenge. History reveals

Macbeth was finally slain by Malcolm Canmore and his men, after a prolonged war for the Scottish crown. According to the chronicles, he was killed in The Peel Ring at Lumphanan, a prehistoric worship site.

that Gruach, Macbeth's real wife, was from an honoured bloodline, and apparently aided in his rule and civil and religious reforms.

DUNCAN Described by Shakespeare as the rightful king, wrongly murdered. The actual Duncan was tyrannical and a destructive leader who foolishly sacrificed large numbers of his men in fruitless campaigns of expansion. He was not poisoned as in Hector Boece's chronicle or murdered as in Shakespeare, but slain in battle during his disastrous campaign against Thorfinn of Orkney. As there was no hereditary kingship, subsequent efforts to 'restore' Duncan's line to the throne were alien to Scottish law and culture.

MACDUFF A Scottish noble according to Shakespeare, who carries revenge and justice to the evil Macbeth who killed his wife and children. In history, Macduff simply does not appear in any early account of the reign of Macbeth, but suddenly springs up in texts from the fourteenth century onwards. He is an entirely fictitious character, who once having entered into a chronicle (the first being John of Fordun in 1384 in which Macduff is merely exiled for his political beliefs) is developed and amplified into the avenger who eventually emerges in Shakespeare's play.

BANQUO A late invention, with no true historical context. First brought into the embellishments of Macbeth's tale by Hector Boece, he was later developed by Shakespeare. The invention of Banquo is political, as he provides an original for the Stuart dynasty. In Shakespeare's case, this type of character would have had a contemporary symbolic value to the monarch James I and VI, as indeed would the whole debate about primogeniture and the inheritance of thrones and power through proven genealogical background.

Holinshed's Chronicles

It is clear by now that the historical Macbeth was a very different person indeed from the character portrayed by Shakespeare. In essence, it must be concluded that the play *Macbeth* and the man Macbeth were totally separate.

Shakespeare drew mainly from Holinshed's *Chronicles*, published in 1577 and 1587. These early history books provided much of Shakespeare's source material for his historical plays, and we can detect a curious bridge between history and drama if we read the chapters of Holinshed that Shakespeare would have used. In the following extracts, which are all taken from the second edition of Holinshed published in 1587, we can detect the fictioinal elaboration which the author developed from earlier chroniclers such as Wyntoun or Boece, whom he undoubtedly consulted. We may also find certain powerful themes, such as the scene with the Three Witches, that have little basis in history, but which made Shakespeare's drama so distinctive.

In reading these extracts, with their original style and period spelling, it is fascinating to consider that these were the words read by Shakespeare before or even as he created his masterpiece. The extracts are the most direct and

Spears of the time (above and opposite), *with decorated silver inlays.*

34

obvious, but scholars have frequently commented that Shakespeare drew material from very diffuse sources; the subtitles before each section are for identification only, and are *not* part of the original text. There is no suggestion here that these are the only parts of Holinshed used in *Macbeth*, but they are those that relate closely to some of the most famous scenes in the play – and that relate also to our true historical Macbeth, so altered through the circumstances of both time and literature.

Duncan and Macbeth

'After Malcolme succeeded his nephue Duncane the sonne of his daughter Beatrice: for Malcome had two daughters, the one which was this Beatrice, being giuen in mariage vnto one Abbanath Crinen, a man of great nobilitie, and thane of the Iles and west parts of Scotland, bare of that mariage the foresaid Duncane; the other called Doada, was maried vnto Sinell the thane of Glammis, by whom she had issue one Makbeth a valiant gentleman, and one that if he had not beene somewhat cruell of nature, might haue beene thought most woorthie the gouernement of a realme. On the other part, Duncane was so soft and gentle of nature, that the people wished the inclinations and maners of these two cousins to haue beene so tempered and interchangeablie bestowed betwixt them, that where the one had too much of clemencie, and the other of crueltie, the meane vertue betwixt these two extremities might haue reigned by indifferent partition in them both, so should Duncane haue proued a woorthie king, and Makbeth an excellent capteine. The beginning of Duncans reigne was verie quiet and peaceable, without anie notable trouble; but after it was perceiued how negligent he was in punishing offendors, manie misruled persons tooke occasion thereof to trouble the peace and quiet state of the common-wealth, by seditious commotions which first had their beginnings in this wise.

Banquho the thane of Lochquhaber, of whom the house of the Stewards is descended, the which by order of linage hath now for a long time inioied the crowne of Scotland, euen till these our daies, as he gathered the finances due to the king, and further punished somewhat sharpelie such as were notorious offendors, being assailed by a number of rebels inhabiting in that countrie, and spoiled of the monie and all other things, had much a doo to get awaie with life, after he had receiued sundrie grieuous wounds amongst them. Yet escaping their hands, after hee was somewhat recouered of his hurts, and was able to ride, he repaired to the court, where making his complaint to the king in most earnest wise, he purchased at length that the offendors were sent for by a sergeant at armes, to appeare to make answer vnto such matters as should be laid to their charge: but they augmenting their mischiefous act with a more wicked deed, after they had misued the messenger with sundrie kinds of reproches, they finallie slue him also.

Then doubting not but for such contemptuous demeanor against the kings regall authoritie, they should be inuaded with all the power the king could make. Makdowald one of great estimation among them, making first a

35

confederacie with his neerest friends and kinsmen, tooke vpon him to be chiefe capteine of all such rebels as would stand against the king, in maintenance of their grieuous offenses latelie committed against him. Manie slanderous words also, and railing tants this Makdowald vttered against his prince, calling him a faint-hearted milkesop, more meet to gouerne a sort of idle moonks in some cloister, than to haue the rule of such valiant and hardie men of warre as the Scots were. He vsed also such subtill persuasions and forged allurements, that in a small time he had gotten togither a mightie power of men: for out of the westerne Iles there came vnto him a great multitude of people, offering themselues to assist him in that rebellious quarell, and out of Ireland in hope of the spoile came no small number of Kernes and Galloglasses, offering gladlie to serue vnder him, whither it should please him to lead them.

Makdowald thus hauing a mightie puissance about him, incountered with such of the kings people as were sent against him into Lochquhaber, and discomfiting them, by mere force tooke their capteine Malcolme, and after the end of the battell smote off his head. This ouerthrow being notified to the king, did put him in woonderfull feare, by reason of his small skill in warlike affaires. Calling therefore his nobles to a councell, he asked of them their best aduise for the subduing of Makdowald and other the rebels. Here, in sundrie heads (as euer it happeneth) were sundrie opinions, which they vttered according to euerie man his skill. At length Makbeth speaking much against the kings softnes, and ouermuch slacknesse in punishing offendors, whereby they had such time to assemble togither, he promised notwithstanding, if the charge were committed vnto him and vnto Banquho, so to order the matter, that the rebels should be shortly vanquished and quite put downe, and that not so much as one of them should be found to make resistance within the countrie.

And euen so it came to passe; for being sent foorth with a new power, at his entring into Lochquhaber, the fame of his comming put the enimies in such feare, that a great number of them stale secretlie awaie from their capteine Makdowald, who neuerthelesse inforced thereto, gaue battell vnto Makbeth, with the residue which remained with him: but being ouercome and fleeing for refuge into a castell (within the which his wife and children were inclosed) at length when he saw how he could neither defend the hold anie longer against his enimies, nor yet vpon surrender be suffered to depart with life saued, hee first slue his wife and children, and lastlie himselfe, least if he had yeelded simplie, he should haue beene executed in most cruell wise for an example to other. Makbeth entring into the castell by the gates, as then set open, found the carcasse of Makdowald lieng dead there amongst the residue of the slaine bodies, which when he beheld, remitting no peece of his cruell nature with that pitifull sight, he caused the head to be cut off, and set vpon a poles end, and so sent it as a present to the king, who as then laie at Bertha. The headlesse trunke he commanded to bee hoong vp vpon an high paire of gallows. . . . Thus was justice and law restored againe to the old accustomed

course, by the diligent means of Makbeth. Immediatlie wherevpon woord came that Sueno king of Norway was arriued in Fife with a puissant armie, to subdue the whole realme of Scotland.'

The Three Witches

'Shortlie after happened a strange and vncouth woonder, which afterward was the cause of much trouble in the realme of Scotland, as ye shall after heare. It fortuned as Makbeth and Banquho iournied towards Fores, where the king then laie, they went sporting by the waie together without other companie, saue onelie themselues, passing thorough the woods and fields, when suddenlie in the middest of a laund, there met them three women in strange and wild apparell, resembling creatures of elder world, whome when they attentiuelie beheld, woondering much at the sight, the first of them spake and said: 'All haile, Makbeth, thane of Glammis!' (for he had latelie entered into that dignitie and office by the death of his father Sinell). The second of them said: 'Haile, Makbeth, thane of Cawder!' But the third said: 'All haile, Makbeth, that heereafter shalt be king of Scotland!'

Then Banquho: 'What manner of women' (saith he) 'are you, that seeme so little fauourable vnto me, whereas to my fellow heere, besides high offices, ye assigne also the kingdome, appointing foorth nothing for me at all?' 'Yes' (saith the first of them) we promise greater benefits vnto thee, than vnto him, for he shall reigne in deed, but with an vnluckie end: neither shall he leaue

The Three Witches or Weird Sisters, first described in Scottish chronicles several centuries after the reign of Macbeth, and later made famous by William Shakespeare. There is no historical evidence that Macbeth consorted with witches. On the contrary, he was a supporter of the established Church.

anie issue behind him to succeed in his place, where contrarilie thou in deed shalt not reigne at all, but of thee those shall be borne which shall gouerne the Scotish kingdome by long order of continuall descent.'' Herewith the foresaid women vanished immediatlie out of their sight. This was reputed at the first but some vaine fantasticall illusion by Mackbeth and Banquho, insomuch that Banquho would call Mackbeth in iest, king of Scotland; and Mackbeth againe would call him in sport likewise, the father of manie kings. But afterwards the common opinion was, that these women were either the weird sisters, that is (as ye would say) the goddesses of destinie, or else some nymphs or feiries, indued with knowledge of prophesie by their necromanticall science, bicause euerie thing came to passe as they had spoken. For shortlie after, the thane of Cawder being condemned at Fores of treason against the king committed; his lands, liuings, and offices were giuen of the kings liberalitie to Mackbeth.

The same night after, at supper, Banquho iested with him and said: ''Now Mackbeth thou hast obteined those things which the two former sisters prophesied, there remaineth onelie for thee to purchase that which the third said should come to passe.'' Wherevpon Mackbeth reuoluing the thing in his mind, began euen then to deuise how he might atteine to the kingdome: but yet he thought with himselfe that he must tarie a time, which should aduance him thereto (by the diuine prouidence) as it had come to passe in his former preferment. But shortlie after it chanced that king Duncane, hauing two sonnes by his wife which was the daughter of Siward earle of Northumberland, he made the elder of them, called Malcolme, prince of Cumberland, as it were thereby to appoint him his successor in the kingdome, immediatlie after his deceasse. Mackbeth sore troubled herewith, for that he saw by this means his hope sore hindered (where, by the old lawes of the realme, the ordinance was, that if he that should succeed were not of able age to take the charge vpon himselfe, he that was next of blood vnto him should be admitted) he began to take counsell how he might vsurpe the kingdome by force, hauing a iust quarell so to doo (as he tooke the matter) for that Duncane did what in him lay to defraud him of all maner of title and claime, which he might in time to come, pretend vnto the crowne.

The woords of the three weird sisters also (of whom before ye haue heard) greatlie incouraged him herevnto, but speciallie his wife lay sore vpon him to attempt the thing, as she that was verie ambitious, burning in vnquenchable desire to beare the name of a queene. At length therefore, communicating his purposed intent with his trustie friends, amongst whome Banquho was the chiefest, vpon confidence of their promised aid, he slue the king at Enuerns, or (as some say) at Botgosuane, in the sixt yeare of his reigne. Then hauing a companie about him of such as he had made priuie to his enterprise, he caused himselfe to be proclamed king, and foorthwith went vnto Scone, where (by common consent) he receiued the inuesture of the kingdome according to the accustomed maner. The bodie of Duncane was first conueied vnto Elgine, & there buried in kinglie wise; but afterwards it was remoued and conueied

38

vnto Colmekill, and there laid in a sepulture amongst his predecessors, in the yeare after the birth of our Sauiour, 1046.'

The Hunterston runic brooch, of Norse–Scottish origin and typical of jewellery favoured by the nobility in Macbeth's time.

King of Scotland

'Mackbeth, after the departure thus of Duncanes sonnes, vsed great liberalitie towards the nobles of the realme, thereby to win their fauour, and when he saw that no man went about to trouble him, he set his whole intention to maintein iustice, and to punish all enormities and abuses, which had chanced through the feeble and slouthfull administration of Duncane. . . . Mackbeth shewing himself thus a most diligent punisher of all iniuries and wrongs attempted by anie disordered persons within his realme, was accounted the sure defense and buckler of innocent people; and hereto he also applied his whole indeuor, to cause yoong men to exercise themselues in vertuous maners, and men of the church to attend their diuine seruice according to their vocations.

To be briefe, such were the woorthie dooings and princelie acts of this Mackbeth in the administration of the realme, that if he had atteined there-vnto by rightfull means, and continued in uprightnesse of justice as he began, till the end of his reigne, he might well haue beene numbred amongest the most noble princes that anie where had reigned. He made manie holesome laws and statutes for the publike weale of his subiects. . . .

These and the like commendable lawes Mackbeth caused to be put as then in vse, gouerning the realme for the space of ten yeares in equall justice.'

Macbeth's Cruelty

But this was but a counterfet zeale of equitie shewed by him, partlie against his naturall inclination, to purchase thereby the fauour of the people. Shortlie after, he began to shew what he was, in stead of equitie practising crueltie. For the pricke of conscience (as it chanceth euer in tyrants, and such as atteine to anie estate by vnrighteous means) caused him euer to feare, least he should be serued of the same cup, as he had ministered to his predecessor. The woords also of the three weird sister would not out of his mind, which as they promised him the kingdome, so likewise did they promise it at the same time vnto the posteritie of Banquho. He willed therefore the same Banquho, with his sonne named Fleance, to come to a supper that he had prepared for them; which was in deed, as he had deuised, present death at the hands of certeine murderers, whom he hired to execute that deed; appointing them to meete with the same Banquho and his sonne without the palace, as they returned to their lodgings, and there to slea them, so that he would not have his house slandered but that in time to come he might cleare himselfe, if anie thing were laid to his charge vpon anie suspicion that might arise.

It chanced yet, by the benefit of the darke night, that, though the father were slaine, the sonne yet, by the helpe of almightie God reseruing him to better fortune, escaped that danger; and afterwards hauing some inkeling (by the admonition of some friends which he had in the court) how his life was sought no lesse than his fathers, who was slaine not by chancemedlie (as by the handling of the matter Makbeth wooould haue had it to appeare) but euen vpon a prepensed deuise: wherevpon to auoid further perill he fled into Wales.'

Macbeth and Macduff

'But to returne vnto Makbeth, in continuing the historie, and to begin where I left, ye shall vnderstand that, after the contriued slaughter of Banquho, nothing prospered with the foresaid Makbeth: for in maner euerie man began to doubt his owne life, and durst vnneth appeare in the kings presence; and euen as there were manie that stood in feare of him, so likewise stood he in feare of manie, in such sort that he began to make those awaie by one surmized cauillation or other, whome he thought most able to worke him anie displeasure.

At length he found such sweetnesse by putting his nobles thus to death, that his earnest thirst after bloud in this behalfe might in no wise be satisfied: for ye must consider he wan double profit (as hee thought) hereby: for first they were rid out of the way whome he feared, and then againe his coffers were inriched by their goods which were forfeited to his vse, whereby he might better mainteine a gard of armed men about him to defend his person from iniurie of them whom he had in anie suspicion. Further, to the end he might the more cruellie oppresse his subiects with all tyrantlike wrongs, he builded a strong castell on the top of an hie hill called Dunsinane, situate in Gowrie, ten miles from Perth, on such a proud height, that, standing there aloft, a man might behold well neere all the countries of Angus, Fife, Stermond, and Ernedale, as it were lieng vnderneath him. This castell, then, being founded on the top of that high hill, put the realme to great charges before it was finished, for all the stuffe necessarie to the building could not be brought vp without much toile and businesse. But Makbeth, being once determined to haue the worke go forward, caused the thanes of each shire within the realme, to come and helpe towards that building, each man his course about.

At the last, when he turne fell vnto Makduffe, thane of Fife, to build his part, he sent workemen with all needfull prouision, and commanded them to shew such diligence in euerie behalfe, that no occasion might bee giuen for the king to find fault with him, in that he came not himselfe as other had doone, which he refused to doo, for doubt least the king, bearing him (as he partlie vnderstood) no great good will, would laie violent hands vpon him, as he had doone vpon diuerse other. Shortlie after, Makbeth comming to behold how the worke went forward, and bicause he found not Makduffe there, he was sore offended, and said: "I perceiue this man will neuer obeie my commandements, till he be ridden with a snaffle; but I shall prouide well inough for him." . . . Macbeth could not afterwards abide to looke vpon the said Makduffe, either for that he thought his puissance ouer great; either else for that he had learned of certeine wizzards, in whose words he put great confidence, (for that the prophesie had happened so right, which the three faries or weird sisters had declared vnto him), how that he ought to take heed of Makduffe, who in time to come should seeke to destroie him.

And suerlie herevpon had he put Makduffe to death, but that a certeine witch, whome hee had in great trust, had told that he should neuer be slaine with man borne of anie woman, nor vanquished till the wood of Bernane came to the castell of Dunsinane. By this prophesie Makbeth put all feare out of his heart, supposing he might doo what he would, without anie feare to be punished for the same, for by the one prophesie he beleeued it was vnpossible for anie man to vanquish him, and by the other vnpossible to slea him. This vaine hope caused him to doo manie outragious things, to the greeuous oppression of his subiects. At length Makduffe, to auoid perill of life, purposed with himselfe to passe into England, to procure Malcolm Cammore to claime the crowne of Scotland. But this was not so secretlie deuised by Makduffe, but that Makbeth had knowledge giuen him thereof: for kings (as is said) haue sharpe sight like vnto Lynx, and long ears like vnto Midas. For Makbeth had, in euerie noble mans house, one slie fellow or other in fee with him, to reueale all that was said or doone within the same, by which slight he oppressed the most part of the nobles of his realme.'

Macduff flees to England
'Immediatlie then, being aduertised whereabout Makduffe went, he came hastily with a great power into Fife, and foorthwith besieged the castell where Makdaffe dwelled, trusting to haue found him therein. They that kept

Decorated sword hilt from the large Viking settlement at Hedeby, Denmark.

the house, without anie resistance opened the gates, and suffered him to enter, mistrusting none euill. But neuerthelesse Makbeth most cruellie caused the wife and children of Makduffe, with all other whome he found in that castell, to be slaine. Also he confiscated the goods of Makduffe, proclamed him traitor, and confined him out of all the parts of his realme; but Makduffe was alreadie escaped out of danger, and gotten into England vnto Malcolme Cammore, to trie what purchase hee might make by means of his support, to reuenge the slaughter so cruellie executed on his wife, his children, and other friends.'

Malcolm Canmore

'At his comming vnto Malcolme, he declared into what great miserie the estate·of Scotland was brought, by the detestable cruelties exercised by the tyrant Makbeth, hauing committed manie horrible slaughters and murders, both as well of the nobles as commons; for the which he was hated right mortallie of all his liege people, desiring nothing more than to be deliuered of that intollerable and most heauie yoke of thraldome, which they susteined at such a caitifes hands.

Malcolme, hearing Makduffes woords, which he vttered in verie lamentable sort, for meere compassion and verie ruth that pearsed his sorrowfull hart, bewailing the miserable state of his countrie, he fetched a deepe sigh; which Makduffe perceiuing, began to fall most earnestlie in hand with him, to enterprise the deliuering of the Scotish people out of the hands of so cruell and bloudie a tyrant, as Makbeth by too manie plaine experiments did shew himselfe to be: which was an easie matter for him to bring to passe, considering not onelie the good title he had, but also the earnest desire of the people to haue some occasion ministred, whereby they might be reuenged of those notable iniuries, which they dailie susteined by the outragious crueltie of Makbeths misgouernance. Though Malcolme was verie sorowfull for the oppression of his countriemen the Scots, in maner as Makduffe had declared; yet doubting whether he were come as one that ment vnfeinedlie as he spake, or else as sent from Makbeth to betraie him, he thought to haue some further triall, and therevpon, dissembling his mind at the first, he answered as followeth:

"I am trulie verie sorie for the miserie chanced to my countrie of Scotland, but though I haue neuer so great affection to relieue the same, yet, by reason of certeine incurable vices, which reigne in me, I am nothing meet thereto. First, such immoderate lust and voluptuous sensualitie (the abhominable founteine of all vices) followeth me, that, if I were made king of Scots, I should seeke to defloure your maids and matrones, in such wise that mine intemperancie should be more importable vnto you, than the bloudie tyrannie of Makbeth now is." Herevnto Makduffe answered: "This suerlie is a verie euill fault, for manie noble princes and kings haue lost both liues and kingdomes for the same; neuerthelesse there are women enow in Scotland, and therefore follow my counsell. Make thy selfe king, and I shall conueie the matter so wiselie, that thou shalt be so satisfied at thy pleasure, in such secret wise that no man shall be aware thereof."

Then said Malcolme, "I am also the most auaritious creature on the earth, so that, if I were king, I should seeke so manie waies to get lands and goods, that I would slea the most part of all the nobles of Scotland by surmized accusations, to the end I might inioy their lands, goods, and possessions; . . . Therefore" saith Malcolme, "suffer me to remaine where I am, least, if I atteine to the regiment of your realme, mine vnquechable auarice may prooue such that ye would thinke the displeasures, which now grieue you, should seeme easie in respect of the vnmeasurable outrage, which might insue through my comming amongst you."

Makduffe to this made answer, how it was a far woorse fault than the other: "for auarice is the root of all mischiefe, and for that crime the most part of our kings haue beene slaine and brought to their finall end. Yet notwithstanding follow my counsell, and take vpon thee the crowne. There is gold and riches inough in Scotland to satisfie thy greedie desire." Then said Malcolme againe, "I am furthermore inclined to dissimulation, telling of leasings, and all other kinds of deceit, so that I naturallie reioise in nothing so much, as to betraie & deceiue such as put anie trust or confidence in my woords. Then sith there is nothing that more becommeth a price than

constancie, veritie, truth, and iustice, with the other laudable fellowship of
those faire and noble vertues which are comprehended onelie in sooth-
fastnesse, and that lieng vutterlie ouerthroweth the same; you see how vnable
I am to gouerne anie prouince or region: and therefore, sith you haue
remedies to cloke and hide all the rest of my other vices, I praie you find shift
to cloke this vice amongst the residue.''

Then said Makduffe: ''This yet is the woorst of all, and there I leaue thee,
and therefore saie: Oh ye vnhappie and miserable Scotishmen, which are thus
scourged with so manie and sundrie calamities, ech one aboue other! Ye haue
one curssed and wicked tyrant that now reigneth ouer you, without anie
right or title, oppressing you with his most bloudie crueltie. This other, that
hath the right to the crowne, is so replet with the inconstant behauiour and
manifest vices of Englishmen, that he is nothing woorthie to inioy it; for by
his owne confession he is not onelie auaritious, and giuen to vnsatiable lust,
but so false a traitor withall, that no trust is to be had vnto anie woord he
speaketh. 'Adieu, Scotland, for now I account my selfe a banished man for
enuer, without comfort or consolation:'' and with those woords the brackish
teares trickled downe his cheeks verie abundantlie.

At the last, when he was readie to depart, Malcolme tooke him by the
sleeue, and said: ''Be of good comfort, Makduffe, for I haue none of these
vices before remembred, but haue iested with thee in this manner, onelie to
prooue thy mind; for diuerse times heeretofore hath Makbeth sought by this
manner of meanes to bring me into hands, but the more slow I haue shewed
my selfe to condescend to thy motion and request, the more diligence shall I
vse in accomplishing the same.'' Incontinentlie heerevpon they imbraced ech
other, and, promising to be faithfull the one to the other, they fell in
consultation how they might prouide for all their businesses, to bring the
same to good effect.'

Malcolm and Siward

'Soone after Makduffe, repairing to the borders of Scotland, addressed his
letters with secret dispatch vnto the nobles of the realme, declaring how
Malcolme was confederat with him, to come hastilie into Scotland to claime
the crowne, and therefore he required them, sith he was right inheritor
thereto, to assist him with their powers to recouer the same out of the hands
of the wrongfull vsurper.

In the meane time, Malcolme purchased such fauor at king Edwards hands,
that *old Siward* earle of Northumberland was appointed *with ten thousand men*
to go with him into Scotland, to support him in this enterprise, for recouerie
of his right. After these newes were spread abroad in Scotland, the nobles
drew into two seuerall factions, the one taking part with Makbeth, and the
other with Malcolme. Heerevpon insued oftentimes sundrie bickerings, &
diuerse light skirmishes; for those that were of Malcolmes side would not
ieopard to ioine with their enimies in a pight field, till his comming out of
England to their support. But after that Makbeth perceiued his enimies power

to increase, by such aid as came to them foorth of England with his aduersarie Malcolme, he recoiled backed into Fife, there purposing to abide in campe fortified, at the castell of Dunsinane, and to fight with his enimies, if they ment to pursue him; howbeit some of his friends aduised him, that it should be best for him, either to make some agreement with Malcolme, or else to flee with all speed into the Iles, and to take his treasure with him, to the end he might wage sundrie great princes of the realme to take his part, & reteine strangers, in whome he might better trust than in his owne subiects, which stale dailie from him; but he had such confidence in his prophesies, that he beleeued he should neuer be vanquished, till Birnane wood were brought to Dunsinane; nor yet to be slaine with anie man, that should be or was born of anie woman.

Macduff kills Macbeth

'Malcolme, following hastilie after Makbeth, came the night before the battell vnto Birnane wood; and, when his armie had rested a while there to refresh them, he commanded euerie man to get a bough of some tree or other of that wood in his hand, as big as he might beare, and to march foorth therewith in such wise, that on the next morrow they might come closelie and without sight in this manner within view of his enimies. On the morrow when Makbeth beheld them comming in this sort, he first maruelled what the matter ment, but in the end remembred himselfe that the prophesie which he had heard long before that time, of the comming of Birname wood to Dunsinane castell, was likelie to be now fulfilled. Neuerthelesse, he brought his men in order of battell, and exhorted them to doo valiantlie; howbeit his enimies had scarselie cast from them their boughs, when Makbeth, perceiuing their numbers, betooke him streict to flight; whom Makduffe pursued with great hatred euen till he came vnto Lunfannaine, where Makbeth, perceiuing that Makduffe was hard at his backe, leapt beside his horsse, saieng: "Thou traitor, what meaneth it that thou shouldest thus in vaine follow me that am not appointed to be slaine by anie creature that is borne of a woman? come on therefore, and receiue thy reward which thou has deserued for thy paines!" and therwithall he lifted up his swoord, thinking to haue slaine him.

But Makduffe, quicklie auoiding from his horsse, yer he came at him, answered (with his naked swoord in his hand) saieng: "It is true, Makbeth, and now shall thine insatiable crueltie haue an end, for I am euen he that thy wizzards haue told thee of; who was neuer borne of my mother, but ripped out of her wombe:" therewithall he stept vnto him, and slue him in the place. Then cutting his head from his shoulders, he set it vpon a pole, and brought it vnto Malcolme. This was the end of Makbeth, after he had reigned 17 yeeres ouer the Scotishmen. In the beginning of his reigne he accomplished manie woorthie acts, verie profitable to the common-wealth (as ye haue heard) but afterward, by illusion of the diuell, he defamed the same with most terrible crueltie. He was slaine in the yeere of the incarnation, 1057, and in the 16 yeere of king Edwards reign ouer the Englishmen.'

GENEALOGY OF CHARACTERS

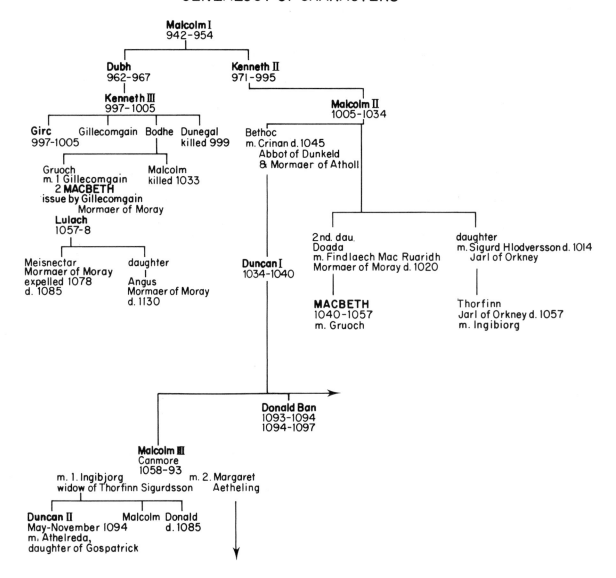

Malcolm I
942–954

Dubh
962–967

Kenneth II
971–995

Kenneth III
997–1005

Malcolm II
1005–1034

Girc
997–1005

Gillecomgain

Bodhe

Dunegal
killed 999

Bethoc
m. Crinan d. 1045
Abbot of Dunkeld
& Mormaer of Atholl

Gruoch
m. 1 Gillecomgain
2 **MACBETH**
issue by Gillecomgain
Mormaer of Moray

Malcolm
killed 1033

Lulach
1057–8

Meisnectar
Mormaer of Moray
expelled 1078
d. 1085

daughter
|
Angus
Mormaer of Moray
d. 1130

Duncan I
1034–1040

2nd. dau.
Doada
m. Findlaech Mac Ruaridh
Mormaer of Moray d. 1020

daughter
m. Sigurd Hlodversson d. 1014
Jarl of Orkney

MACBETH
1040–1057
m. Gruoch

Thorfinn
Jarl of Orkney d. 1057
m. Ingibiorg

Donald Ban
1093–1094
1094–1097

Malcolm III
Canmore
1058–93

m. 1. Ingibjorg   m. 2. Margaret
widow of Thorfinn Sigurdsson   Aetheling

Duncan II   Malcolm   Donald
May–November 1094   d. 1085
m. Athelreda,
daughter of Gospatrick

Further Reading

Dorothy Whitelock (ed) *Anglo-Saxon Chronicle* London, 1961

W.M. Hennessy (ed) *Annals of Loch Ce* Dublin 1871

B. MacCarthy (ed) *Annals of Ulster* Dublin 1887–95.

Wilson, D. *Archaeology and Prehistoric Annals of Scotland* Edinburgh, 1851

Rev. John Williams Ab Ithel (ed) *Brut Y Tywysogion* (Rolls Series) London, 1860

A&B Rees, *Celtic Heritage* London, 1961

W.F. Skene, *Celtic Scotland* (3 Vols) Edinburgh 1886

W.F. Skene (ed), *Chronica Gentis Scotorum, De Fordun,* (14th C) Edinburgh 1871

Holinshed, *Chronicles of England, Scotland and Ireland*, London, 1577

B. Thorpe, (ed) *Chronicon ex Chronicis, Florence of Worcester* London, 1848

G. Wutz (ed) *Chronicon, Marianus Scotus,* 1844

R.F. Walker, *Companion to the study of Shakespeare's Macbeth* London, 1947

Dr. A. Ross, *Folklore of the Scottish Highlands* London, 1976

J. Stevenson (ed), *Historia Dunelmensis Ecclesiae* 1855

Hector Boece, *Historia de Scotia*, Paris, 1527

W. Blackwood, *History of the Celtic Place Names of Scotland* Edinburgh, 1926

Lloyd Laing, *Late Celtic Britain and Ireland*, London, 1977

J. MacBeth, *MacBeth, King, Queen and Clan* Edinburgh, 1921

William Shakespeare, *Macbeth* various editions

R. Carruthers, *Macbeth, being an Historical figure* Inverness, 1930

Alexander Burt Taylor (ed), *Orkneyinga Saga* Edinburgh, 1938

Dr. A. Ross, *Pagan Celtic Britain* London, 1974

Bannatyne Club, *Prioratus Sancti Andree in Scotia*, 1841

MS 23/G4, Royal Irish Academy, *Prophecy of St. Berchan* Dublin.

Andrew Wyntoun, D. Ley (ed), *The Orygynale Cronykil of Scotland* Edinburgh, 1879

J. Graham Campbell, *The Viking World* London, 1980

Illustrations

Colour plates by James Field

All line illustrations by Chesca Potter

Map and diagram by Chartwell Illustrators

Photographs courtesy of: Chris Lloyd/National Portrait Gallery, Scotland (page 29); Peter Newark's Historical Pictures (pages 33 and 42); Scottish Tourist Board (pages 13, 18, 24, 28 and 31).

Index

Page numbers in *italics* refer to illustrations.